LAWS TO LIVE BY
STEPS TO A BETTER LIFE

DR. STEVEN A. JIRGAL

Published by The Core Media Group, Inc., P.O. Box 2037, Indian
Trail, NC 28079.

Printed in the United States of America.

LAWS TO LIVE BY
STEPS TO A BETTER LIFE

Our lives are surrounded by laws. We have traffic laws, federal laws, state laws, financial laws, physical laws, and a host of other laws that time or space does not allow us to mention. We understand the importance of these laws although we may not appreciate them. They add order, safety, and progress to our lives without which we would face escalating difficulties. Imagine what life would be like if everyone was allowed to drive at any speed and in any manor they desired. What if nobody was punished for crimes they committed? Suspend the law of gravity even for one hour and think of the chaos it would create.

Just as there are laws governing our physical and civic lives, there are general laws that govern our personal lives. Violation of these laws creates personal problems as well. Following are ten laws that will maintain order and foster success in our lives.

You Become What You Are Surrounded By

One of the endearing qualities of a chameleon is its ability to blend in to its surroundings by changing color. For the chameleon, this is an involuntary adaptation. Socially, you and I will adapt to our surroundings as well. We will speak, act, and adopt the values of the people with whom we spend the most time. This will be true throughout our lives regardless of our age. With few exceptions, the people we come in regular contact with will either bring us up or bring us down. They will cause us to grow or decline in character. We will become the average of our five closest associates. This brings us to a choice: do our friends exhibit the characteristics we want exemplified in our lives? If not, the only option is to change our surroundings.

Ella and Kari were high school friends. They played basketball and soccer together and were both in the drama club.

They went to separate colleges and began to develop friends on their respective campuses. Ella found herself among the students that were serious about their studies. She worked hard in her classes and by the time she graduated she had made the dean's list five times.

Kari, on the other hand, gravitated toward those who saw college as a playground. She drank almost every weekend and even experimented with drugs. Due to some very poor decisions she too was on the dean's list. At the end of her sophomore year she was dismissed from the university. She never got her degree and struggled with alcohol her entire life.

Surround yourself with good people and you will become like them.

The Choices You Make Today May Determine the Opportunities You Have Tomorrow

Life is full of choices. Some of them make little difference while others are monumental. What color car you drive, where you go to dinner, or the style of your hair bears little or no significance in your life. Other choices you make can be life changing. Business deals, personal relationships, and financial decisions can be life altering.

Jim enjoyed his time with his friends. They welcomed him, accepted him and always provided alcohol for him. He never worried about drinking and driving because he had never been caught even though he had done it a number of times. So on a particular night he said good-bye to his friends and staggered to his car. Then the predictable happened. He took a curve too fast, lost control and crashed into a tree. The impact left him paralyzed from the neck down. No longer would he go to work. No longer would he go hunting. No longer would he drive a car. After about a year in the wheel chair being totally dependent on others, his body gave out and he died.

Tom worked as a programmer for a medium sized manufacturing company. While driving to lunch, he turned the corner to see an elderly woman trip and fall on her driveway. Turning his car around he chose to go back and ensure that she was okay. When he reached the woman he found that she suffered only scrapes and bruises and just needed some help in getting into her home. He left his business card after being assured that she was alright. Two days later, Tom was summoned into his boss's office. The owner of the company wanted to know about the incident. Tom explained wondering how his boss knew about it. He learned that the woman, overwhelmed by his concern and kindness called the company to relay the incident. Leaning forward, his boss said, "Tom, we appreciate your kindness towards someone who couldn't pay you back, so we've decided to pay you for her." Then he slid a gift card to an expensive restaurant across the desk in his direction.

As a freshman in college, John made a string of bad choices one Saturday night. His mother was out of town, so he chose to host a party at their home. Even though he was underage, he chose to serve his friends alcohol. He chose to put the party on social media and before long the house was packed with many people he had never met. He chose to be violent with one of them sending the stranger to the hospital. He was arrested and charged with assault, underage drinking, disorderly conduct, and serving alcohol to minors. Aside from the fines, lawyer fees, and court costs he will have to pay, he is no longer eligible for a position in law enforcement and will forfeit his life-long dream of working for the FBI.

Choices bring consequences. Choose wisely!

People Will Forget What You Say
and People Will Forget What You
Do, but They Will Never Forget the
Way You Made Them Feel
-Maya Angelou

Feelings are important. The person who said, "Sticks and stones may break my bones, but names will never hurt me" was not at the receiving end of that scenario. A kind word, a held door, name recognition, and a personal note of encouragement go a long way toward nurturing a person's heart and lightening their load. The good news comes from two points: 1-To make someone feel appreciated and valued takes very little effort and costs very little time and money. 2- you can start today with anybody in which you come in contact.

William Arthur Ward said, "Flatter me and I may not believe you. Criticize me, and I may not like you. Ignore me, and I may not forgive you. Encourage me, and I will not forget you. Love me, and I may be forced to love you."

-4-

Time Is Limited

❧

"Time and tide wait for no man." Time marches on with or without your consent. The new year is ushered in whether or not we watch the ball drop in Times Square. We all may be different in many ways. Some are richer than others. Some have more talent than others. Some have other advantages over others. But one thing every member of the planet has in common with everyone else: we all have twenty-four hours granted to us each and every day-no more, and no less. Along with this idea of time is the truth that we each will come to the end of our days on earth. Father time is undefeated and all roads lead to the cemetery. No one gets out alive! So the question remains: what will you do with the time you have?

In the movie *Braveheart*, the character William Wallace is leading his Scottish warriors against a horde of English soldiers. As they prepare for battle he makes a statement that we would do well to note, "Every man dies. Not every man lives."

The following writing by S.H. Payer should serve

to put in perspective the use of the gift we are given each and every day.

"This is the beginning of a new day. God has given me this day to use as I will. I can waste it or use it for good. What I do today is important, because I'm exchanging a day of my life for it. When tomorrow comes this day will be gone forever, leaving in its place something I have traded for it. I want it to be gain, not loss: good not evil: success, not failure. In order that I shall not regret the price I paid for it because the future is just a whole string of nows.

Time is limited! Count your days and make your days count!"

The Real Measure of a Person Is Their Character

We evaluate each other in so many ways. Cars, homes, bank accounts, the beauty we were blessed with, and a host of other things are all means by which we size up one another and determine "Who's Who" in our world. However, some make great doctors but poor neighbors. Others know how to make money but can't make friends. Still, others can fix machines but they can't repair their marriage or family. Where is the disconnect in all of this? It falls in the area of character. Of all that makes up a person's life, character is the one element that truly lasts.

Integrity, kindness, generosity, loyalty, commitment, love, dependability, and countless other character traits are what is left when everything else fades from view.

Horace Greeley once said, "Fame is a vapor, popularity an accident, and riches take wings. Only one thing endures and that is character."

Character counts. Have you counted yours lately?

Happiness Is a Choice

❧

Happiness is an emotion. And like all other emotions we can choose to embrace it or stifle it. Too often we buy the lie that people and things will make us happy. So we spend our life in futility chasing the approval of people and the gathering of things. Then when we have endured the dizzying ride on this merry-go-round with people we find we don't care for we discover that the brass ring we've spent all our energy trying to grab is rusty and not worth holding on to.

Stuart was a successful businessman who was recruited by a company to transfer his talents and his clients to their firm. He made the move with the promise of a large financial bonus. He waited for his bonus for weeks. Each day he went to work wondering if this was the day his big check would arrive. Several times each week he asked if the check had been cut. Finally, he received the long awaited bonus. He stared at the check for some time. It was a lot of money, but somehow it didn't deliver the satisfaction he was counting on. He gave a heavy sigh and made the comment, "I thought it would be a bigger deal to me." Stuart had made the mistake in thinking that things would bring him happiness.

For three months Stacy lived with a family in South America. She worked with them, played with them, and immersed herself in their culture. She relates the fond memories she has of spending each night with the family singing and laughing as they watched the sun go down on another day. She comments fondly, "I've never met anyone who could have so little and yet be so happy." They have learned that happiness is found in who you are, and who you're with, not in what you have.

Abraham Lincoln said, "Most folks are as happy as they make up their minds to be."

Happiness is a choice that is independent of what we have or who we know. Have you made the choice to be happy?

The Scoreboard Is Not the Only Measure of Victory

It is possible to lose in competition and be satisfied because of your effort. It is equally possible to beat your opponent and not be happy because you know you have not done your best. Winning or losing is determined by effort not score. Victory is found in putting forth your very best effort and fighting to the very end despite the scoreboard.

Vince Lombardi coached the Green Bay Packers from 1959-1967. His Packers won the first two super bowls ever played and in all his years coaching on the professional level he never had a losing season. He said, "The price of success is hard work, dedication to the job at hand, and the determination that whether we win or lose, we have applied the best of ourselves to the task at hand."

No matter what the scoreboard reflects, if you do your best, play within the rules, and don't quit, you can lay your head on your pillow each night and rest with the satisfaction that winners alone enjoy.

-8-

Wisdom Is a Precious Commodity

Wisdom is attainable and will aid you in your quest for success. It will keep you out of trouble and save you time, energy, and money. With wisdom life simply gets better. But not everyone you meet can be labeled wise. Categorically people fall into three areas: Fools, smart people, and wise people.

A fool is easy to spot. He is constantly making the same mistakes. He seems to be forever broke, bruised, and blaming his situation on everyone else. Because he refuses to learn from others and even his own experiences, he is destined to suffer the repercussions of his poor decisions.

Smart people make mistakes (we all do), but they learn from their mistakes. Their memory is good and they are determined not to fall in the "same hole" again.

Wise people however, understand that there is not enough time to learn from all the mistakes you need to make in order to avoid them. They study the lives of others, see the mistakes others have made and learn from them. Those who are wise listen. They ponder and consider. They give attention to the task at hand with the information they've attained.

Wisdom is just like any other commodity. It can be obtained. It can be shared. It can be used to make your life better. Pursue wisdom and watch success follow.

People Matter More Than Things

Though it may be referenced, you'll find that very little time is spent eulogizing a person's possessions. When it comes down to a funeral, what matters most is mentioned most. Interpersonal relationships are talked about more than anything else. The reason for this is very simple, people matter more than things.

This is well illustrated by a story attributed to Joann Jones:

> *During my second month of college, our professor gave us a pop quiz. I was a conscientious student and had breezed through the questions, until I read the last one: "What is the first name of the woman who cleans the school?" Surely, this was some kind of joke. I had seen the cleaning woman several times. She was tall, dark-haired, and in her fifties, but how would I know her name? I handed in my paper, leav-*

ing the last question blank. Just before class ended, one student asked if the last question would count toward our quiz grade.

"Absolutely," said the professor. "In your careers, you will meet many people. All are significant. They deserve your attention and care, even if all you do is smile and say, 'Hello.'"

I've never forgotten that lesson. I also learned her name was Dorothy.

People show appreciation-things do not.

People receive and give love-things do not.

People communicate-things do not.

People bring long-term peace and comfort-things do not.

People share ideas, dreams and goals-things do not.

People instruct us and challenge us to higher ideals-things do not.

People need people-things do not.

People matter more than things. Are you spending your time with that which matters most?

Progress Is Made Through Struggle

When a caterpillar is in a chrysalis it is in the process of developing into a butterfly. When the time is right, it begins to emerge very slowly and deliberately. Over a long period of time with much struggle it breaks free of its shelter, flexes its wings and flits off to a new life as a thing of beauty for all those around to enjoy. But there is so much more to the story than that. As the butterfly is struggling to free itself it is performing a very important exercise. The struggle for freedom is strengthening its muscles and empowering it to fly. Further, the action of pushing against the chrysalis is pressing important chemicals out to its wings giving it the vibrant color it later displays. The struggle itself brings strength and beauty. Without this important step the butterfly would be severely weakened, its colors would miss their brilliance and its life would be truncated.

The same is true of us. Too often we avoid hardships. But difficulty is what brings about our strength and progress. When you speak to couples that have been married for several years and ask about their early years, often they will bring up the struggles they endured. They have learned that these obstacles they faced and overcame brought resilience to their marriage and character to their souls.

An unknown writer penned these words:

> *Looking back, it seems to me,*
> *All the grief that had to be,*
> *Left me when the pain was O'er,*
> *Stronger than I was before.*

Weight lifters get stronger by lifting weights not by reading articles about lifting weights. It is in overcoming trials and set-backs that we grow. No man can be successful until he is willing to hurt himself deeply. The pain of the journey to success brings about strength to be used for further progress.

Closing Thoughts

Years ago, an experiment was done involving elementary school children. The children were observed during recess. Around the perimeter of the school yard a fence was constructed. The fence came to represent restrictions placed upon the children. Unconsciously they saw it as an inhibitor to freedom and fun. They climbed the fence, pushed against the fence, and even tried to run around the fence to "freedom."

· After a period of time, the fence was removed and the children were observed again. Those involved in the experiment noticed that the children would play during their recess time, but their walking, running and playing were considerably closer to the school. Without knowing it the children's view of the fence had changed. The fence that had at one time stood for the infringement of their ability to enjoy freedom and fun, came to represent safety and security.

What is true of children is also true of us. The above laws of life can bring to your mind the loss of pleasure and freedom. But if they are viewed correctly, they can stand for success and enjoyment. The choice of which viewpoint you want to adopt is and always will be yours to make.

About the Author

❧

Dr. Jirgal is a 1980 graduate of Gettysburg College where he became a four-time conference champion, All-American, and inductee to the Middle Atlantic Conference *All Century Team* in the pole vault. He holds an undergraduate degree in health education and physical education. Following graduation, he taught on the high school and college level while coaching football and track in both venues. He holds masters degrees in health education, sports medicine, and divinity, as well as a doctorate in ministry.

He has been the director of Sports Medicine at Wingate University, area director for the Fellowship of Christian Athletes and has served on the staff of Hickory Grove Baptist Church in Charlotte, N. C., as well as leading Lakeview Baptist Church, in Monroe, N. C. as the Senior Pastor. He has served on the local board of directors for the Fellowship of Christian Athletes, New Orleans Baptist Seminary and the ministerial board of Wingate University. He currently serves on the board of directors for

The Carolina Study Center, and Fathers in Touch ministry.

Dr. Jirgal is the founder and director of *The Jirgal Leadership Institute* where he strives to equip people for success in leadership roles. He and his wife Pam have three children, Joshua, Caleb, and Sarah. They reside in Monroe, N. C.

OTHER BOOKS BY DR. STEVEN JIRGAL

The Path of a Champion
Dirty Dozen
Dying to Live
Life Points
Principles of Wholeness
Mining the Mind of King Solomon

**To learn more about the titles above,
visit www.JirgalLeadership.com.**

www.ingramcontent.com/pod-product-compliance
Lightning Source LLC
Chambersburg PA
CBHW060605030426
42337CB00019B/3616